LEARNING TO SWIM WHEN YOU'RE SCARED:

How To Overcome A Fear of Water

Katie Smith

Learning to Swim When You're Scared:
How To Overcome A Fear Of Water

Illustrations by Emma Wright

Contact: katieswimguides@yahoo.com.au
Website: www.katiesswimmingguides.weebly.com

ISBN 13: 9780992436360
ISBN 10: 0992436362

CONTENTS

STARTING OUT

If you want to learn to swim, jump in the water. On dry land no frame of mind is ever going to help you.

BRUCE LEE

INTRODUCTION

Hello and welcome! If you are reading this book I presume you are a non-swimmer who would like to learn to swim. I'm also presuming the reason you haven't yet learnt to swim is because you are scared of the water (anywhere from a little bit all the way to terrified).

I am an Austswim qualified swimming instructor who has worked with hundreds of scared adults during my ten years in the industry. I have witnessed the joy they experience when they finally conquer a long-held fear and discover the fun and freedom that swimming provides. Yet I also realise that many people are hesitant to enrol in swimming classes because they are scared or embarrassed to do so. To that end, I have to say to learn the formal swimming strokes (freestyle etc) I highly recommend attending at least some 'in person' swimming classes. It is not something I believe I can teach you in a book. **So, the purpose for this guide is not to teach you to swim 50 metres of freestyle or backstroke, but rather to get you to the point where you can confidently get in the water and participate in a class (or have a friend or relative teach you).**

The main emphasis of this guide is getting you comfortable with submersion as I believe it to be the thing most non-swimmers are afraid of. Once you can confidently submerge, you will be much more open to attempting the other physical manoeuvres necessary for swimming. (If you can already comfortably submerge but are still afraid of the water this guide may not give you the answers you are seeking).

There are many reasons adults have missed the opportunity to learn the skill of swimming and have thus developed a fear of the water. Perhaps you grew up in a cold climate and simply had no opportunity to swim in your childhood or maybe your town didn't have a public swimming pool. It could be that your parents were non-swimmers and passed this mantle onto you. Or, more than likely, you had a scary experience(s) in the water at some point which freaked you out so much you've avoided donning a swimsuit ever since.

Whatever your reason, no matter how old you are, how unfit or overweight or how long it's been since you even put a toe in the water – you CAN overcome your fear of the water and learn to swim. I'm not promising you it's going to be easy, but it certainly isn't overwhelmingly difficult or unachievable. The most important thing you need at this point is a genuine desire to overcome your fear of the water and a personal commitment to expend the required time and effort necessary to achieve this goal.

If you can already get in the water without feeling scared and can put your face under, then this guide will probably not be challenging enough for you and enrolling in a learn to swim class right now while you have the motivation to do so is my recommendation.

I suggest you read right through this guide a few times before starting your journey from non-swimmer to swimmer. Familiarise yourself with the steps involved and prepare yourself for the journey ahead. As previously mentioned, all you need at this point is a desire to overcome your fear and the motivation to follow through. Oh, and you will need regular access to a swimming pool of some kind.

I cannot offer any guarantees of success, but I do genuinely believe if you follow the steps set out you will gradually conquer your fear. This is not a magic cure or an easy fix – it is merely the information you need to succeed. It is up to you to follow the steps and I really hope you will do so. The very fact you've picked up this book suggests to me that you want to learn and that is the first element in mastering any new skill.

All right then! Let's get started. You are about to discover what I believe to be one of life's great joys – the sport of swimming.

Why indeed? There is no reason you have to swim if you don't want to. I am not suggesting you are any less a person if you can't swim and have no desire to do so. But the fact you are reading a book about overcoming a fear of the water suggests that you DO want to learn to swim. There could be any number of reasons for this – perhaps your kids or grandkids are taking classes and you don't want to get left behind, maybe you're sick of sitting on the sidelines during family events at the beach or you might be planning a cruise or a world trip and want to be able to experience some of the great oceans our planet has to offer. Or maybe it's just an item on your bucket list that you want to conquer. It doesn't matter why you want to learn – all that matters is that stating your desire has taken it from a vague, fuzzy dream to a real, concrete goal.

To me swimming and being in the water is one of life's greatest pleasures. My "perfect day" would include at least one swim (preferably early morning in a tropical ocean) and I can't imagine my life without aquatics in it. I understand that not everybody shares my passion and I'm not trying to "convert" you to being as infatuated with the water as I am. But I do have to say that most people I come across who say they don't enjoy swimming, or the water, are not great (or even good) swimmers. They are usually not comfortable in the water and while they may be able to do a very basic swimming stroke, they are just not confident away from terra firma.

Naturally there is a logical link between these two things – to be a good swimmer you need to spend a fair amount of time in the water. So it stands to reason that non-swimmers and weak swimmers have not spent much time in the water and thus haven't really had an opportunity to develop a true feel for the water. Therefore you will probably need to push through some early fear and uncertainty until you get to the point where you can judge if you actually dislike the water and swimming or if you are just scared and unconfident.

I will share a personal story with you at this point. When I was growing up in sunny Queensland, I loved to go swimming at every opportunity – be it at the local pool, my cousin's pool or at the beach. While my siblings and Dad always got in the water my mother never did. She always had a reason – she'd just washed her hair; she didn't like the salt water or she couldn't supervise us properly if she was in the water too. Eventually we stopped asking her and came to conclusion that she just didn't enjoy swimming. It wasn't until I was in my twenties that I realised she *couldn't* swim. My eldest brother and his wife had just started taking their twin sons to swimming lessons. Given that you needed a parent in the water with each child and the class was on a weekday when my brother was at work my sister-in-law asked Mum if she would be the other "parent". I'm not sure what it was about Mum's face at that point, but I suddenly got it and realised she couldn't swim. I could see that she desperately wanted to help her grandchild but was simply unable to. As often happens in life once the made the admission a string of serendipitous events occurred eventually leading Mum to a newly opened swimming centre that specialised in adult classes. Once she got going, she was unstoppable. She and Dad even installed their own pool (my siblings and I couldn't believe the injustice of this after spending our whole childhood begging for our own pool).

My mother will be the first to tell you if she could do it anybody can. She did struggle to start with but doggedly kept at it, absolutely determined she would be able to get in the water with her beloved grandchildren. Like any skill some people are more natural than others, but anybody can learn if they want to.

WHAT ABOUT LESSONS?

So, you might ask – why not just enrol in lessons now? What is the point of this book? Good questions! If you feel you are ready to do that then go right ahead. I highly encourage it. But I get the feeling you aren't yet ready – that's why you're reading a book about overcoming a fear of the water. Because, let's face it, if you were truly ready to take swimming lessons, you would have done so by now. It is totally OK that you're not ready, by the way – that is why I have written this book, to help you get to the stage where you are ready to enrol in lessons.

Besides that, there is a more practical reason to undertake the exercises in this book before you start swimming lessons. It comes down to simple mathematics and also value for money. If you wish to start swimming lessons as an absolute beginner, swim schools can and do cater for that. However, your lesson will only be between thirty and sixty minutes. You will probably only have one or two lessons per week. As a very scared beginner it may take you months to progress through the more difficult early stages of overcoming a water fear. It will add up both in financial terms and time outlay. You may have a specific timeframe in which you want to learn to swim (maybe a special holiday or other occasion), or you might have just decided you want to get on with it and don't want to spend months not making a lot of progress. The exercises outlined in this book can move you through the early stage in a relatively short period of time, provided you are prepared to practice very regularly to begin with.

Another cost consideration to consider might be that as an absolute beginner you would only feel comfortable in a private one on one lesson (that will cost you more). If you can get yourself to a stage where you are happy to participate in a group lesson, you will save yourself a lot of money and also make friends with people who are in the same place you are in terms of swimming ability.

The other option is to enrol in lessons but also undertake the exercises in this book in tandem, which should speed up your progress even more. As I said before I do recommend lessons, but only when you feel ready.

WHAT ABOUT PHYSICAL/MEDICAL ISSUES?

If you have any ongoing physical or medical issues you should check first with your doctor or health care professional and get a clearance to swim.

Provided you have the right support, there are very few conditions that will not allow you to get into the water and try swimming. Even if you cannot walk, you can still swim. Obviously, you would need to modify some of the exercises and would need assistance getting in and out of the water, but this can be arranged. Many pools have hoists for those who cannot walk.

FORGET THE NEGATIVES

One of the most common things would-be learner swimmers say is, 'I'd love to take swimming lessons but...'

- I'm too old
- I'm too overweight
- I'm afraid to put my face under water
- The water gets up my nose
- I don't like cold water
- The pool is too crowded
- Other people will laugh at me
- It's too expensive
- I'm not a sporty person

Just to name a few!

All of the above may seem like valid reasons but in reality they are just excuses. If you genuinely want to learn to swim little things on the above list will not stop you. To start with you are never too old. There is no such thing as an upper age limit for adult swimming classes. As long as you can get in the water you can learn. The same goes for being overweight. No pool I know has an upper weight limit and if you are overweight you will actually float much easier than a slim person. Sure, you might be self-conscious about putting on a swimsuit, but I can honestly assure you that people of every shape and size regularly visit pools, the beach or the river.

Look for a flattering swimsuit that covers as much as possible and forget about everybody else.

As for cold water, I don't like it either – the good news is that almost all public pools these days are heated once the outside temperature drops below a certain level. Even better is that the smaller teaching pools and children's areas (which you are totally entitled to use) are even warmer (generally around 32 degrees Celsius or 90 degrees Fahrenheit). Or failing that you could go to a totally indoor centre (there are lots of them around) which will be guaranteed to be warm. (See section on heated/non heated pools on page 16).

I do agree a crowded pool can be daunting but there is a way around this. Ask the pool staff when the quietest times are. Having worked at a pool for many years I can guarantee you that there are times when the pools are almost empty. Early morning and later in the afternoon are often great times or the mid-afternoon (after morning classes but before afternoon ones start). Many pools will even have a timetable that sets out what happens at certain times. Just ask, they will be happy to tell you.

I can't guarantee that nobody will laugh at you, but I can assure you it's pretty unlikely. First of all, if you go at a quiet time there won't be very many people to even see you let alone make fun. Secondly most people are far too involved in their own dramas to worry about you. Find your own little space and do your own thing. As for people laughing at the idea of you learning to swim, that says far more about them and their own insecurities than you stepping up and conquering one of your own fears. Forget about them!

Pool fees can get expensive if you are visiting a lot – but there are ways to minimise this. First of all, you don't always need to go to a public pool. I will outline suggestions later on that don't even involve a pool or you may have a friend or family member who will let your use theirs. Public pools do have multi-use passes – either weekly, monthly or yearly. They may seem a lot of money up front but when you work out how much cheaper each visit is, they are worth it. They also allow unlimited entry, so for example you could come two or three times per day if you wanted to. It might mean giving up a take-away coffee or another luxury, but it will be worth it to achieve your goal. Check also for pension/concession/senior or student discounts.

For those worried about not being athletic or sporty I will say here what I say to a lot of parents when they bring their children for swimming lessons. Not everybody is a natural swimmer, but everybody can learn to swim. When I say a natural swimmer, I mean somebody who has an inbuilt ability or talent. Just like there are natural singers or pianists or natural writers or artists. Any of these skills can be learned and pursued by others too – you just won't progress as fast or as easily. Is this a reason to give up? No, it isn't. Remember the story of the hare and the tortoise. The tortoise got there in the end, and you will too if you continue to put in the effort. Human beings can float and move through water – it has been proven over thousands of years of civilisation. You are not the sole exception to this rule.

Let's face it, any of the above may sound like valid reasons for not conquering your fear, but deep down we both know they are excuses. If you really want to learn, you won't let anything stand in your way. So again, just to be clear I am not suggesting you are any less a person if you genuinely don't want to learn to swim. If you don't want to swim, just accept it, put this book aside and continue to live your life without swimming in it. If you do want to learn, banish all the negatives from your mind and start genuinely believing you CAN do it. Because you can!

SUPPORT PERSON

As you embark on your journey to learn to swim, I **strongly** suggest you find yourself a support person (at least for the early stages). This can be a family member or a friend but most of all it needs to be somebody you are completely comfortable with and who won't get bored a few lessons in and leave you to your own devices. Remember they will see you at your most vulnerable so select them wisely. A calm person who doesn't panic easily is the way to go.

Your support person is there to help and encourage you but also for your safety. Public pools do have lifeguards, but they have a lot of people to watch. You want somebody who can stay by your side the whole time and guide you as necessary.

Choose somebody who is a good swimmer and completely comfortable in the water. Have them read this guide before they start so they know the process. Don't choose somebody pushy or impatient who will hound you to 'just do it!' You want this person with you for safety and support, not to challenge or scare you.

Your support person will also keep you accountable. You will obviously need to arrange times with them to work on your swimming skills, meaning it is much less likely that you will chicken out if only relying on your own motivation to go to the pool.

HEATED VS NON-HEATED POOL

Whether you choose to swim in heated or non-heated pool largely comes down to personal preference and climatic conditions. Unless you live in a very hot climate almost all public pools will be heated in the cooler months. Outdoor pools will generally seem cooler than indoor (even if the water temperature is the same). There are a couple of reasons for this. Most obviously is that outdoor pools are affected by air temperature, wind and rain and also the steam from the heated water is quickly dissipated. Because you will only be partially submerged, especially in the earlier stages, you may feel cold if it is windy and wet parts of your body are exposed to the wind. Indoor pools can control their air temperature (either through air-conditioning or heating), and this has a big impact on how the water feels. Even if you are partially submerged in an indoor pool, you are unlikely to feel cold because the air temperature will be comfortable and consistent, and you won't have to worry about wind or rain.

The over-riding factor you want to take into consideration when choosing which type of pool to swim in is personal comfort. Different people tolerate water temperatures in different ways. Growing up in a warm climate I struggle when it comes to cold water, but those from cooler climates think nothing of swimming in water that give me goose bumps. When first learning to swim you will not be moving around a lot, so your body will not warm up like somebody exerting themselves by swimming laps. So you will need to take this into consideration, as your body is affected by extremes in temperature and you will be more prone to cramps if your core temperature is lower than normal. The time of day can also play a part in being too cold. For example, late afternoon in autumn after the sun has gone off the water or when afternoon breezes roll in can be much colder than the morning.

Don't be put off by the idea of swimming in winter, it can actually be the best time to work on learning to swim if you have access to a heated pool.

Public pools tend to be much quieter in the winter, providing you with a wider choice in times and space. You are also much less likely to be bothered by children running and jumping around you. The main consideration with winter swimming is keeping yourself warm before and after you get wet. Rug up as much as you need to until the moment you have to get in the water. This may include a beanie and ugg boots, as keeping your head and feet warm is important. A swimming/deck coat is ideal for winter swimming. Designed to be worn before and after your swim (even when wet), it allows you to stay warm without having to dress in layers of clothes. Getting in the water is the hardest part, once in and warmed up you will be reluctant to get out again. Once out of the water warm up with a nice hot shower and get dressed in your dry clothes as quickly as possible.

PRACTICE, PRACTICE, PRACTICE
(BUT GET IT RIGHT FIRST)

When learning a something new, it can be tempting to try and rush ahead through the skills, even if you haven't quite mastered the one before. This is only normal when you are excited and enthusiastic about what you are learning and/or if you have a timeframe in mind for when you want to have mastered whatever it is you are learning (in this case, swimming). However, you will need to override this temptation as you learn to swim, or your progress will be impacted.

With each of the skills I have outlined in this guide, you need to get them right and practice them a lot before you move onto the next step. This could mean un-learning some old habits you may have picked up in your previous experiences with swimming – for example swimming with your head out of the water, kicking incorrectly or not blowing bubbles under the water. Your brain already has entrenched neural pathways where your previous swimming habits (if any) reside. The great news is that you can build new pathways, but the old pathways will remain and will revisit as

17

soon as you let them. If you take the time to practice a new skill thirty times, you will train your brain to keep that skill up. If you decide to just practice five times, you may start out well but will soon drop back to your old habit as your body tires and goes into survival mode. Instead of staying on the new pathway your brain will default to the old shortcut that requires less physical and mental energy.

Yes, it can be boring and frustrating to keep things short and repetitive when you are enthused about learning to swim and just want to make progress, but, like any swim teacher will tell you, it's the only way forward. Doing only minimal practice of a new skill is a waste of your time and will ultimately leave you frustrated. Bunker down for the early sessions and nail those core skills and you will be ready to tackle each new step with confidence.

It is also important to keep working on the previous skill as you take on each new one. There's no point in getting skill number one right but letting it fall by the wayside when you get to skill number two. It's a constant building process as you go forward, which is why it's best to take your time instead of trying to rush through.

VISUALISE

Before you begin the journey to learning to swim, go somewhere where you can watch people swim – it could be your local public pool, the beach or swimming hole, or a friend's pool. Or you could even watch it on TV or on the internet. What you want is to get a sense of how relaxed people are in the water. Swimming is an activity that people do for relaxation and enjoyment as well as fitness. As a human being you are capable of that same sense of relaxation and freedom you will see from competent swimmers. Watch children and the way they play in the water – you too can experience that same playfulness. All you need is to develop the basic skills that will unlock your swimming potential.

Now I want you to picture yourself in the water enjoying it like the people you are observing. See yourself walking confidently into the pool complex or onto the beach with your towel, eager and ready to get into the water. That is the goal you are chasing, and you need to make it a real and vivid image in your mind. Revisit that image as often as you can – several times a day at least. Stick with me and you will get there for real.

CHAPTER CHECKLIST

★   Make the decision to learn to swim!

★   Choose a Support Person

★   Get your mindset right by dismissing any negative preconceived ideas

★   Have a medical check-up if required

★   Commit to regular and consistent practice

★   Visualise yourself swimming!

WHY AM I SCARED?

You cannot be so afraid to sink that you forget you have the ability to swim.

SOPHIA REED

Before you even go anywhere near the water you need to ask yourself **why** you are scared. Once you understand and acknowledge that reason you will have conquered your first major hurdle in this process. Below are some common reasons:

- Lack of exposure to water throughout your life resulting in little or no experience
- A cultural reason (eg you grew up in a country where swimming was not considered appropriate for women)
- Missing out on the basics in childhood which has resulted in a lack of confidence and a continued avoidance of swimming throughout your life
- A frightening incident at some point in your life that scared you so much you've kept away ever since (this could be a personal experience or one you witnessed)
- Parental anxiety passed onto you
- A genuine phobia that brings about physiological symptoms (eg panic attack or nausea). This can be triggered by a traumatic experience with water/swimming or sometimes it's just the outward manifestation of another deeper unknown fear.

The first three reasons are the least difficult to overcome. This is simply because a fear of the unknown is a normal human reaction to an unfamiliar situation. It is how I feel about ice-skating for example. I'd quite like to try it but the thought of it scares me because I don't have the skills required and I'm worried I would hurt myself if I fell over. I realise though that after some lessons I could become proficient. I would be nervous to begin with but would eventually get over that fear. And the more I practised the better I would get at it.

Think about some of those reality TV shows where celebrities undertake some kind of challenge – for example Dancing With The Stars. This show takes people with very little or no experience in ballroom dancing and has them undertake a rigorous training regime in a fairly short space of time. When you watch clips, you can see how each celebrity progresses from pretty much making a fool of themself to becoming reasonably proficient or even very good. Most are very nervous and unsure to begin with but gain confidence as they practice, fail, practice, practice and so on. I'm sure if you asked any of them after their very first attempt, they would not be confident of mastering it. Sure, they are lucky to have professionals on hand to help and guide them, but the process of improvement is the same – there are no magic shortcuts.

You can do that with swimming. You may not have had experience with it in the past, but you can now dramatically increase your exposure to it, and you will start to improve as <u>you</u> practice, practice, practice.

IDENTIFY YOUR FEAR

Even if you already know why you are scared of swimming, you need to write it down to formalise in your mind where the fear comes from. Once you have done that you can make a plan to move forward. Writing it down is as simple as:

I am scared of swimming because I grew up in Ireland in a small town where there was no public swimming pool. Nobody in my family could swim and it was not something that bothered me until I moved to Australia and realised most people here can swim and it is an important part of the culture.

Next, write down why you want to learn to swim. Once again this is fairly simple:

I want to learn to swim because my children have had lessons and love the water and it is something that looks very enjoyable. I want to make the most of the warm climate and enjoy cooling off on a summer's day. I also want to exercise more and it seems like a gentle way to get fit.

The second three reasons for being scared are more complex but it doesn't mean you *can't* learn – not at all! It just means you will have to take some additional steps to overcome your fear.

ANALYSE YOUR EXPERIENCE

For those who have been freaked out by a scary experience in the water, you need to take a step back and do a post-mortem of what happened. This will allow you to be objective about it and (hopefully) move on from it. This might seem like an unnecessary step, but it is very beneficial. Even if you're sure it won't help, humour me and do it.

Firstly, you need to write down exactly what happened to you. This may sound silly, but it is really helpful. Take a piece of paper and make some notes. Put in as much detail as you can – such as your age, where you were, what other people were involved and the physical impact. Below is an example. ¨

"I was seven years old and playing with my friends at the local public pool. I could swim a little bit but not well enough to get out of my depth. There were no adults supervising us. Then one of the big kids came over and threw me in the deep end. I felt myself sinking to the bottom and started swallowing water. No matter how much I tried, I couldn't get back to the top. Just when I thought I was going to die another swimmer pulled me up and back to the side. I coughed up lots of water and vomited several times but nobody really made much of a fuss about it and the kid who did it didn't apologise. I had nightmares about it for weeks afterwards and I have hated swimming ever since."

It is completely understandable that such an incident would cause a fear of the water. Obviously this person from the example above never had anybody take them aside at the time and talk them through the incident and then gently coax them back into the water and gradually rebuild confidence. As the years went on the fear continued to manifest and when they were old enough, they just made the decision to stay away from the water.

Now I want you to look at this incident through the eyes of an adult and try to be objective about it. Most people reading this would agree that it wasn't the water itself that was the problem or the pool. It was the action of an irresponsible person. The pool/water did not make you sink, it was because you were small, obviously couldn't swim properly and were put in a situation that was well outside your control.

It may sound trite, but you need to forgive the other person for the horrible thing they did to you and make the decision to move not only past it but well beyond it. Decide that you will no longer let your experience of the water be clouded by a long-ago incident that would not have happened in a perfect world. I realise that doing this will not make your fear magically disappear and allow you to suddenly jump into the deep end of the nearest pool but, believe me, it will help at least a little bit. It is also a concrete, non-threatening first step you can take in the journey of overcoming your fear without having to go anywhere near a pool. You have probably felt ashamed or embarrassed about your fear of water and seeing the reason written down can be quite cathartic and allow you to acknowledge that there are genuine reasons for your fear and that you should stop feeling bad about it.

If your scary incident happened in another kind of waterway, such as the beach or a river or creek you have some other things to consider. In that case the environment played a part – either by current or a rip or a sudden change in depth, or perhaps there was some hidden object that posed a danger. Reassure yourself that this time you will be swimming in a pool, which is a much more controlled environment. You will NOT be at the mercy of any outside elements and will be able to choose depth and temperature. You will be able to see the bottom and it will be firm underfoot. Further reassure yourself that you do not have to ever swim in a natural water source again if you don't want to. However, once you are confident in a pool you may well consider trying again. But it is not something you need to think about yet.

Of course there could be any number of situations that freaked you out, (there could actually be more than one) but you get the idea. Write it down, analyse it and revisit it with adult wisdom. Draw a line under that old memory and get ready to create a new mindset.

For those of you who have a genuine phobia of the water, this will also require more work, but it is definitely something you can overcome. A phobia is a very deep, irrational fear about something specific (in this case water) that causes you to (a) go to great lengths to avoid it and (b) experience a physiological reaction in your body. This could be a full panic attack (eg sweaty palms, pounding heart, hyperventilation) or other symptoms such as dizziness, a dry mouth or nausea. A person with a phobia will experience these symptoms even if there is little or no danger from the thing or situation in question. (Yes, it could be said water can be dangerous, but in a normal, controlled environment it is not). It is thought that about ten percent of the population have a phobia at some point of their lives, and most are aware of it. If the thought of getting in the water causes severe anxiety and you make a conscious choice to avoid it all costs, I would suggest you get some professional help or at least read and research overcoming phobias.

Getting professional help does not have to be an expensive, drawn-out process. Your GP should be able to refer you to a professional who deals with phobias, this can be a hypnotherapist, a psychologist or even a psychiatrist. Treatment for a specific phobia by any of these professionals, generally using cognitive behavioural therapy, can be quick and the results amazing.

I am not saying you have to do this, but I do suggest thinking carefully about it. It can take weeks or months of constant exposure to even get as far as putting your feet in the water if you are truly phobic. (And even then you still might not be comfortable with it). However, with professional treatment you can eliminate a huge chunk of this timeframe. Support groups led by a professional can also be very beneficial for overcoming phobias.

Other alternative treatments such as kinesiology and acupuncture can also help pinpoint physical triggers for anxiety in your body and help eliminate them. They are certainly worth considering. I cannot endorse or guarantee they will help you but based on personal experience and anecdotes from different students they can do wonders if you go in with an open mind.

If neither of those suggestions appeals or they are not practical for you, do some research on phobias and gain an understanding of why you are afraid and what you can do about it. Check on the internet or use your local library. There will be a psychology section that will have information about phobias. Although they can be debilitating, phobias are one of the better understood aspects of human psychology. In very simple terms phobias are generally treated by gradual and safe exposure to the thing or situation you are affected by. Of course there is a proper process for this, which is why you should read further and gain more understanding before trying any kind of self-treatment.

There are also many websites such as www.hypnosisdownloads.com that address very specific fears and phobias, including fear of water. Of course you should be careful to choose only reputable sites and this is only a suggestion, not a promise of an instant cure.

CHAPTER CHECKLIST

★   Identify your fear(s) and write it down – there could be more than one reason

★   Analyse why you are afraid, reflect and make a plan to move on from the old fear

★   If it is not a phobia continue on

★   If it is a phobia, consider treatment or further research to help you overcome it

★   Visualise yourself swimming!

FIRST SPLASH

When you swim you don't grab hold of the water, because if you did you would sink and drown. Instead you relax and learn to float.

ALAN WATTS

I am going to move through the steps to successful submersion right from the beginning. If you are a little more advanced, you can skip through some steps until you get to the point where you need help.

The very first thing we need to work on is water on the face and you don't need to go anywhere near a pool to work on this. Start in the shower – have the water at a comfortable temperature and place your face directly under the stream. Close your eyes and your mouth and just let the water run over your face. How does that feel? Are you okay with it or does it make you uneasy or even a little panicky?

If you don't like water on your face, ask yourself why. Is it the sensation of the water or the thought that you can't breathe properly with water running over you? Or is it a real feeling of panic? If you are truly panicked, you may have a water phobia. Refer back to the advice above about phobias. You can also undertake the steps below, but just be aware it may take you longer to move through them. Stick with it though and you will eventually get there.

The best way to overcome a feeling of being uncomfortable is to continually expose yourself (in a safe way) to the situation in question until it eventually becomes more comfortable. Before beginning this process remind yourself that water is a natural element that will not hurt you. Coming out of the shower head it cannot build up to a level that will pose any kind of danger – it is simply running right off you and down the drain. You can breathe even with water running over you and the best way to avoid inhaling water is to keep your breathing relaxed and even. It is only when you breathe heavily in a panicked fashion that you will take water into your mouth or nose.

Start with a short burst – say one second. Repeat this at least three times during your shower. The next day increase it to two seconds and increase the repetitions. Gradually work your way up to at least five seconds with at least ten repetitions. By this stage you should feel fairly relaxed with it. If not, continue for a few more days until it really is completely comfortable. There is no time limit on this exercise – take a couple of weeks if you need it. You really do want to be completely comfortable with water on your face before we move to the next stage.

You can also practice this exercise in the bath or in a pool. If you are in the bath, sit comfortably in the water. If you're at a pool either sit on the side with your legs in the water or on the steps/shallow ledge with just your legs submerged. Cup your hands and then dip them under the water. Then splash the water from your cupped hands onto your face. Make sure your eyes and mouth are closed and that you don't inhale through your nose. Do it ten or twenty times each session until you are completely relaxed with the process. Another option is to fill a sink with water and try it that way. Make sure the water is a pleasant temperature for your own comfort.

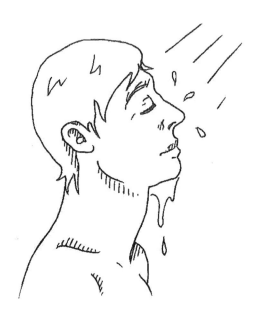

Why are we focusing so much on submersion? Wouldn't it be easier to dip your toes in then the rest of your body? Well, yes, it might be easier initially, but for most non-swimmers putting their head under is the thing they are most afraid of. Once we can conquer that fear you will be much readier to do the other physical manoeuvres required without the constant worry that your face will somehow end up under the water.

Remember I have worked with adults for many years and I have tried the toes in first approach without any emphasis on submersion. In all honesty it takes much longer. There are really no swimming movements that will keep your face completely dry and, also, those afraid of submersion will develop an incorrect habit to avoid it. (I am amazed sometimes just how people can contort their body to avoid their head going under!).

By avoiding submersion, you might learn how to do a form of freestyle with your face out of the water, (which takes quite a while as it's very awkward). You are also constantly anxious about your head going under accidentally. When you do finally submerge, however, you would then need to re-learn the correct freestyle technique. Like any bad habit, incorrect swimming technique can be very hard to correct. Not to mention the time and effort wasted in the meantime.

If you genuinely want to learn to swim you need to embrace submersion. Wouldn't you much rather go the whole hog instead than just half-heartedly 'sort of' learning to swim? Besides all that, swimming really is much more fun when you go under – if you don't submerge you are only getting half the enjoyment, not to mention missing out on much easier movement in the water. (Trust me it is very difficult to swim for any kind of distance with your head above the water and it puts a huge strain on your neck muscles).

BUT I'M REALLY SCARED…..

Why are people so afraid of submersion? Well, there are several reasons.

Obviously we are not designed to breathe under water so any time spent under the water is limited. It is not an instinctive thing for a human being to do. So most people would say they are afraid of running out of air, pure and simple. Other reasons include the fear of swallowing water or inhaling it through the nose or getting it in their eyes. Let's address those fears.

<u>Running Out Of Air</u> – yes, you will run out of air if you stay under the water too long. However, when you swim you learn how to float and move through the water which allows you to lift your head and take a breath. As long as you periodically lift your head out of the water and take a breath you will not run out of air. When you are still learning you will stay in shallow water where you can touch the bottom, so at any point you can stand up to take a breath. Don't worry, we are going to work through this gradually in a way that will leave you in complete control.

<u>Fear of swallowing water or inhaling through the nose</u> - every swimmer has done this and yes, it is not pleasant. But it's not that bad either. Sure, you may cough or have some discomfort in your nasal passages for a few seconds – but it won't kill you. Besides all that there are very simple steps you can take to prevent either of these things happening. The key to prevent swallowing/inhalation of water is to NOT inhale when you are under the water. You will learn to blow bubbles a bit later down the track, but to start with not inhaling is as simple as keeping your mouth closed and not breathing in through your nose. This can be a bit of a mental hurdle because somebody who is scared will often instinctively inhale deeply. So as added insurance you could block your nose with your fingers or even wear a nose clip when you're starting out. (You can then gradually wean yourself off it as you go).

<u>Water in the eyes</u> – I agree it is not always pleasant to get water in your eyes, especially when the water is strongly chlorinated or very murky (if swimming in open water). The best way to address this is to wear goggles. They will protect your eyes from the elements and allow you perfectly clear vision under the water. If your vision is not good and you usually wear

prescription glasses or contact lenses, you can get prescription goggles to wear in the pool. Check with your optometrist to do this.

Make sure you get a good quality pair of goggles that fit correctly. They will cost a bit more but will do what you need them to do. Cheap goggles often leak and/or the straps break easily. Go for well-known brands such as Speedo, Zoggs or Vorgee. Contrary to popular belief goggles do not need to be tight. The strap should sit comfortably around your head and should not feel like it is digging in. When putting your goggles on, hold them against your eyes to start with. You should feel a gentle suction that will hold them against your face. Then pull the strap around. If you have to stretch the strap hard it is too tight. Also, if you end up with deep red marks around your eyes then your goggles are too tight. Goggles can have clear, tinted or mirrored lenses, which one you choose is personal preference. If you swim indoors, there is no real need for tinted lenses, for example. Some brands also have male and female versions, this will also come down to personal preference and your face shape and size. Follow the manufacturer's directions to get the best result from your goggles.

A common issue with goggles is that they can fog up after a certain time in the water. This can happen with even the most expensive brands (that claim not to fog up). However there is a simple solution to prevent this problem. Get yourself a small bottle of baby shampoo. Before putting your goggles on put a tiny drop in each goggle lens and smear it around with your finger so the lens is coated. Then simply rinse the goggles thoroughly (either under the tap or in the pool itself). Put the goggles on as usual and you will remain fog free while you swim. Taking measures to prevent fogging before you swim will prevent a lot of frustration and the need to remove and rinse your goggles while swimming.

Note: at some point you should practice without goggles just so you get used to not always having them on – however for the purposes of this book (which is to prepare you for formal swimming lessons), I believe we should use every possible advantage to make you as comfortable as possible in the water. So I would strongly suggest you get some goggles.

CHAPTER CHECKLIST

★   Prepare for the idea of submersion, it's a necessity when you are learning to swim

★   Start preparing for submersion in the shower with water on your face

★   Use goggles, they will remove a lot of anxiety, protect your eyes and allow you to see clearly

★   To prevent getting water up your nose don't inhale. Use a nose clip if you are anxious about this to start with.

★   Relax and breathe, this should be fun

TESTING THE WATER

Believe you can and you're
halfway there.

THEODORE ROOSEVELT

Now it is time to actually get into the pool. While it might seem scary, it is also an exciting step. Before we start there are a few steps to prepare. Getting these things organised before you start will remove potential extra layers of anxiety that may let you procrastinate for longer.

WHAT TO WEAR

It's a great idea to invest in a good quality swimsuit before you get in the pool. This means a chlorine resistant fabric. While it may be more expensive than Lycra, it will last ten or even twenty times as long. All the major brands have chlorine resistant ranges. While sun safety is important, it is much easier to swim without being weighed down by rash vests, t-shirts or long board shorts. They really do increase the drag in the water and that is not something you want to worry about when you are learning. Try to choose a time when the sun is not too strong or use an indoor or shaded pool if possible. If you do need to wear a rash vest, make sure it fits snugly.

For women just a plain one piece with sturdy straps is perfect, or if you choose a two piece make sure it's a sporty style rather than a bikini or tankini. You want to concentrate on your swimming, not on what your swimwear is doing! If you are body conscious, choose a style that covers well (for example you can get women's swimwear with built in arms, legs and/or high neck and back). If you have cultural considerations in regard to swimwear, you can get long tights and long-sleeved tops to keep you covered. Just make sure they are firm fitting as any loose clothing will drag in the water. Make sure too that it is light fabric, as heavier materials will get waterlogged and feel heavier. Remember, too, that once you are in the water and moving nobody will pay attention to what you are wearing.

For men either the Speedo style briefs, or the knee length trunks are best. Long board shorts will act like a parachute in the water. You want to concentrate on your swimming, not be annoyed about your boardies billowing around you.

A **swimming cap** is also a good idea for women (unless you have very short hair). Not only does it keep your hair out of your eyes and mouth, it will also help protect your locks from at least some of the ravages of chlorine. A cap also makes it much easier to put your goggles on and off. (In addition, if you wear goggles without a cap, your hair will get a lot of breakage along the goggle line. Ask any hairdresser if you don't believe me!). Men can also wear a cap if they choose – but because their hair is generally shorter (or non-existent in some cases), it's not a necessity. The best kind of swimming cap to get is a silicone one as it will last years with proper care and is the easiest to get on and off. While they are the most expensive up front (although still relatively cheap), a silicone cap will easily outlast any other kind. A lycra/cloth cap is kinder to your hair and will have a fair life span but with continued use the elastic and fabric will degrade and become stretched and loose. A latex cap is the cheapest and the least user friendly. Latex caps tend to be harder to put on, are tighter around the edge (sometimes uncomfortably so) and rip easily. They also tend to deteriorate when stored for any length of time. Having said all that though the choice is ultimately yours. Swimming caps tend to be one size, but some brands do offer a larger size which is best for women with long hair who need to put it up under the cap. There is a bit of a learning curve when putting your swimming cap on, but you soon get the hang of it. With proper care (rinse and dry after use) a quality swimming cap should last for several years.

ENTRY AND EXIT

This may seem too basic a thing to talk about, but it is something you want to be totally comfortable with when you start swimming. Also depending on the setup of the pool it can be stressful for a beginner to deal with. The best entrance/exit is a set of steps with a hand rail in the shallow end of the pool which allow you to easily walk in and out of the water. This allows you complete control when you get in and out of the pool. Unfortunately, not all pools have this, so we will also discuss other entrances and exits you may have to contend with.

Some pools will only have ladders for entry/exit. If that is the case, there are a few tips to help you feel safe and in control when using it. Firstly, take your time. If other people are crowding around, let them go first, so you can go at your own pace without feeling pressured to hurry. Make sure you grasp the ladder with both hands and only climb down/up one rung at a time. (The ladder should be firmly attached to the pool wall, if it isn't tell pool staff so they can get it fixed). When climbing into shallow water from a ladder hold onto it until both feet are firmly on the ground. When climbing out grasp the ladder with both hands with your feet still on the ground before taking your first step up. When you get to the top, continue holding onto the ladder with both hands until both feet are firmly on the pool edge.

It would be unusual for a public pool to not have steps or a ladder, but some private pools may not have either. This may seem a little scary, but there are still safe ways for a beginner to get in and out. If the water is quite shallow (up to waist height) and if you are comfortable to do so, you can sit on the side of the pool with your feet in the water. Place both hands firmly on the pool edge on either side of you and gently lower yourself feet first into the water. If you don't like the sound of that, you can sit on the side, then roll onto your tummy and gently lower yourself in that way. It's not the most elegant move but it is safe and effective.

Getting out can be a little trickier, but not too difficult. If the water is fairly shallow (up to waist depth) stand with your back against the wall and place both hands firmly on the pool edge and hoist yourself up until your bottom is on the pool edge. Then you can swing your legs around and stand up that way. If you have reasonable strength in your arms and are comfortable doing so, you can go out face first. Stand with both feet firmly on the bottom and both hands on the pool edge. Then use your arm strength to hoist yourself out of the water. Depending on how agile you are, you can either lift yourself onto your knees or your feet. This way can be a bit tough on your knees, so perhaps you could either lay an old towel down before you get in the water or have somebody put one there for you just before you get out. Another option if you are using a private pool is that you may be able to place some kind of step into the pool to assist you (for example a milk crate weighed down with a couple of bricks works well).

Overall, take your time and make sure you have a firm hand/foot hold before attempting entry and exit if you are not totally confident in the water. Also always enter/exit in the shallowest part of the pool.

GETTING A FEEL FOR THE WATER

The very first thing you can do around a pool is to simply sit on the edge and dangle your feet in the water. Move them backwards and forwards and notice how the water flows easily around. You can also dip your hands in the water and have a little splash. Focus on staying calm and getting used to the smell of chlorine and the noises around the pool. Watch other people swimming and rather than feeling envious, simply observe the way they swim. Watch the way they kick or how they position their head. Most importantly watch how relaxed they are and keep this in your mind as you think about swimming yourself.

If you know of a pool with a beach style entry this is an ideal and very safe way to *gradually* familiarise yourself with water. Start slowly – walk down into the water until knee depth and then sit down. Lie on your back in the shallowest part and feel the water lap around you without it splashing over you. Wriggle down a little further if you're happy to. Feel the water around your ears – notice how it runs in and out without any discomfort. Move around in the water and experiment with kneeling and sitting. Get used to the feel of the water around your body. Lean back on your elbows in the shallowest part and allow your feet to rise up. Kick them up and down. You can also do this on your tummy – rest on your bent elbows and lift your feet up. Although designed for children, shallow entry pools are a great way to introduce yourself to the water. Just copy what they kids do.

You can gradually inch your way down into deeper water, until you are sitting in chest deep water. Just sit for a while and feel the water around your body. You can also continue to splash yourself periodically with water, just to keep up that skill.

In a regular pool enter safely into shallow water where you feel safe and stable and walk around. Hold onto the side to begin with and then move a little distance away as you gain more confidence. Have your support person stay close by but try as much as you can by yourself. It is an unusual feeling to begin with, especially if you have not been in a swimming pool for a long time (if at all). You will notice you cannot walk fast in water, there is resistance.

In waist depth water practice bobbing up and down. This does not have to be fast, and you do not have to put your head under the water. Start out by holding onto the side or have your support person hold your wrists or forearms and support you as you lower yourself in the water (to neck depth). You will notice how much easier this is under the water than on dry land! Once you have bobbed down, stand up again, taking as much time as you need. Splash yourself periodically, both on the face and the rest of your body. Keep calm as you do this and breathe in a relaxed way.

If your support person agrees and you feel confident enough, you can also explore the deep end of the pool. Place your fingers on the pool edge and move along slowly. You will notice the water getting gradually deeper. When you can no longer touch the bottom, just keep grasping the edge – your hands will easily support you. Move your hands along the wall and you will keep moving. Notice how the water easily supports you – you do not need to hold on for dear life and there is no stress on your hands to keep you afloat. Always keep your support person close by when you are doing this but do what you feel you are capable of. Push your boundaries a bit if you feel confident enough.

CHAPTER CHECKLIST

★ Invest in a good quality swimsuit, goggles and a cap (if required)

★ Scope out the entry/exit and practice getting in and out of the pool until it is stress free

★ Use a shallow water entry pool if you can

★ Practice the suggested water familiarisation exercises until you feel comfortable in a pool setting – this may take or one two sessions or it might take ten

★ Relax and breathe, this should be fun

TAKING THE PLUNGE

Skill comes from consistent and
deliberate practice.

SHAWN ALLEN

All right, now we are getting down to the nitty gritty. We are going to start putting our face under water (still water that is, not the shower). Before you begin, make sure you are very comfortable in a pool setting as you do not want to carry unnecessary anxiety into learning submersion. If you are still a bit shaky getting in the water, go back a step and work more on the water familiarisation skills. There is no fixed time frame for gaining confidence and as I mentioned earlier, you do not want to try and move onto a new skill until the previous one has been mastered.

There are several ways you can learn submersion. We will start with the most obvious which is a pool. Make sure you have your support person with you and that they understand what you are aiming to do.

It is very helpful if you can sit – be it on the steps, on a ledge or in the shallowest part. If you are at a public pool, see if they have a children's play area. These often have a graduated beach style entry where you can sit comfortably. If not a play area, see if they have a teaching pool with a shallow ledge (most will). If you are in a larger pool, choose one with steps you can sit on if possible (without impeding other people getting in and out of the water). Once again this is where you need to be careful about choosing your time. Talk to the pool staff and find out when the quietest times are (early morning and later in the evening are often the best times for the children's area or teaching pool. If your pool doesn't let the public use the teaching pool talk to the staff and explain what you are doing – they will probably be more than happy to let you use it as long as you have someone with you).

If there is not an area where you can sit safely, stand in the shallow end (which should only be waist to chest deep). Have your support person standing right next to you and hold onto the side firmly with both hands. If there is a rail along the edge hang onto it.

If you are using a private pool, try and sit if you can – the steps are often the only option here. Or perhaps you could put some kind of ledge in the water that you can sit on. Just like the public pool if you need to stand, hang onto the edge firmly and have your support person right next to you.

Right, so you are in the water sitting/standing comfortably. You are in control and you are stable in the water. You should have your goggles on and your nose clip (if you need it). Make sure you are relaxed first by taking some deep breaths. When you are feeling calm, take a breath and hold it, then dip your mouth in (keep it closed) and lift it out again. Relax for a few seconds and take another breath, then go again.

Once you have mastered mouth only, dip your mouth and your nose in (hold your nose if you need to). It is the same motion; you are just dipping a tiny bit deeper, like the picture below.

Next you are aiming to put your face in the water (not your whole head yet). Count yourself down from three, take a breath and hold it, and just dip your face in the water for half a second. Think of your face as a circle in line with your ears. Remember keep your mouth closed and do NOT inhale through your nose. (Hold your nose if you need to). After half a second lift your face out.

There you go! You did it! See, it's not too scary is it? Sit back and relax for a minute – you've just taken the first step to conquering your fear. Well done! Aim to do the face dip at least twenty times in your first session (maintaining the half second timespan and then increasing it gradually as you go along – up to five seconds).

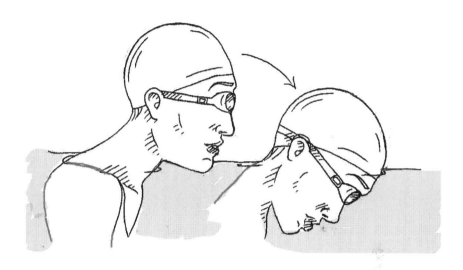

For the rest of the time in the water, continue familiarising yourself with the feel of it – move around and experiment. Get your support person to help you if necessary. If you are confident enough, go for a walk across the shallow end (holding onto the side if you need to). If you are still very scared just sit/stand and get used to the sensation of the water around your body. Move your arms backwards and forwards and make little waves. See how the water flows around your body.

As I said, you will need to keep practising this until you are completely comfortable with it for at least five seconds at a time (longer if possible). This may take days or even weeks, or you may conquer it in just one session. It doesn't matter how long it takes, just keep doing it until you're okay with it. Remember the more you practice the faster your progress will be. Every day is fabulous if you can manage it – or at least three times per week (at this stage of the learning process). If you started out holding your nose or using a nose clip, try and wean yourself off that before you move on to the next skill. Remember at this stage you don't want to breathe in or out while under water. I promise you the only way water will go up your nose is if you breathe in. So again, it may mean lots and lots of practice, but you will get there as your confidence grows.

OTHER OPTIONS FOR SUBMERSION

Okay, what if you can't use a pool for submersion practice? Either because you don't have one accessible, you don't want to spend the money on admission for short sessions or because you're just not confident enough to get in one yet? Fear not, there are other ways you can practice your submersion skills, all of which you can practice in the privacy of your own home.

The first way is to use either a large bowl, bucket, plastic tub, sink (kitchen or laundry), it can be anything as long as it is big enough to dip your face (and eventually your head) in. It should be a comfortable fit – you don't want to get your head jammed in there or injure yourself.

Choose a time when you are not going to be interrupted (as you may feel a little self-conscious – if you don't mind other people seeing you then it doesn't matter when you do it). Fill the vessel with water (preferably warm but it's up to you). Wear your goggles and your nose clip if you need to. Now either stand, kneel or sit and practice the same submersion skills outlined above. Take a breath and hold it, (hold your nose if you need to), and dip your whole face in the water. Start out with just half second intervals and gradually increase as you get more confident.

If you are able to leave the vessel of water in place for several hours or a whole day, I would recommend you do so. (Please only do this if it is **safe**. If you have small children in the vicinity do **NOT** leave any kind of uncovered water in an accessible place). Continue to practice your submersion several times per day. Perhaps you could do it every hour. This may seem like overkill, but it will boost your confidence at a much faster rate. Remember the more you expose yourself to a situation, the more relaxed you will become with it. Don't get disheartened if it seems to take a long time to extend your submersion intervals – just keep plugging away and you will get there. Make sure you are relaxed before you start and give yourself a decent break between plunges into the water.

A third option for submersion practice is the bathtub or, (don't laugh), a wading pool. If you choose the bath, you will need to have it full enough so that you can get your face in the water without having to contort your body too much. It is best if you can be sitting comfortably and just lean forward. Don't put any bubble bath, bath salts or shampoo in the water until you've done your practice. Follow the same directions as above and practice daily if possible. Use your goggles (and nose clip if necessary).

A wading pool is a great tool for practising submersion. They are not terribly expensive (if you just get a basic one) or you could look on second-hand sites like Gumtree or eBay or at garage sales. Even if you do buy a new one you can look on it as an investment in overcoming your fear of water and can always resell it yourself later. You want to get a wading pool that is large enough for you to sit comfortably and at least 30 centimetres (one foot) deep. Remember you will be able to use it further down the track too so a larger one is good if you can manage it.

Undertake the same exercises as detailed above. Depending on where you live and where you put the wading pool, will determine what temperature you want the water to be. Remember even if you live in a warm climate, you don't want the water to be freezing. Given that a wading pool can use a reasonable amount of water you don't want to have to empty and fill it up every time you use it. Check out some accessories such as mini-filtration systems and covers (both to keep the water warm and to keep leaves, dirt and other debris out). Another option is to set up your wading pool indoors if you have the space and the right kind of flooring (cement or tile). A garage is a good option too. With a wading pool you have the option of practising several times a day – do this if possible. It will speed your progress up. Like any kind of pool though, you must be vigilant about safety. You will either need to keep the wading pool in a securely locked or fenced area or covered so that no child can access it.

When you are comfortable submerging your face for at least five seconds, you are ready to move onto the next skill.

WHOLE HEAD UNDER

You should now be able to submerge your face in the water for at least five seconds. Congratulations for making it this far! You have done some of the hardest parts of the process – you started and you submerged your face. The fact you are reading about the next step indicates that you are ready and willing to move on. I'm so pleased for you. If you haven't already done so give yourself a little treat of some kind to celebrate.

If you are using a nose clip or holding your nose, now would be a great time to try and wean yourself away from that. Try the exercises in the previous section again without blocking your nose. Remember the key to prevent water up your nose is to NOT inhale. It really is as simple as that. Good on you if you can let your naked nose in the water. Don't fret if you can't just yet. You can move onto the next stage with a blocked nose, but just bear in mind you are moving towards leaving behind your nose clip. Swimming really is much easier without having to physically block your nose. But as I said that can come later. At this stage we just want you under the water any way you can.

Putting your whole head under is not that different to submerging just your face. All that is required is for you to push your face a little deeper into the water so that your whole head is under. Remember you are still safe and stable in the water, so it does not need to be scary.

If the idea of getting water in your ears bothers you, consider using ear plugs or a swimming cap to keep your ears covered. However, unless you have some particular problem with your ears, submerging them is painless, it can just take a little getting used to. Sure, water will flow in, but it will flow out again just as quickly when you lift your head back above the water. It can feel a bit strange to start with, but just bear with it and soon you won't even notice it. Remember at this stage you are still keeping your mouth closed. You do not need to clench your mouth closed tightly, just keep your lips firmly together.

You can go back to two second intervals to begin with (if you feel you need to). Start just like facial submersion but keep gently pushing until your whole head is under and then quickly lift it back out again. Give yourself time to recover and then take a breath and go again and again. Gradually increase your time under water up to at least five seconds – if you're brave try for seven or even ten seconds. You can keep the interval between submersions a bit longer if you feel you need to but as you get more relaxed, you will probably find you will only need a fairly short rest.

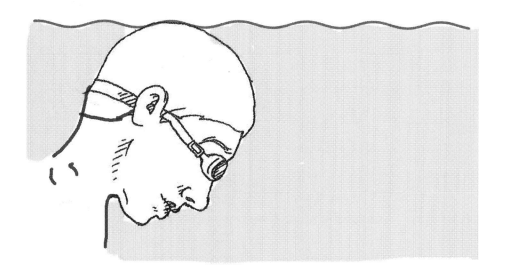

If you are a ready for a bit more of a challenge, you can try bobbing your head under the water vertically rather than going in face first. There are a couple of different ways you can do this. If you are in shallow water hold firmly onto the side with both hands (hold the rail if there is one) and simply lower yourself into a squatting position until the top of your head is under the water. Start with two seconds under again and work your way up to longer intervals. Or you could hold onto the hands of your support person and try the same thing. Gripping them around the wrist is probably the most secure way to keep you stable as you bob down.

Alternatively you can move into deeper water (about chest to neck high) and try the same thing. You will not have to squat down as far this time. Just hold the side firmly and bend your knees until the top of your head is underneath the water. Hold for two seconds to start with and then work your way up to five.

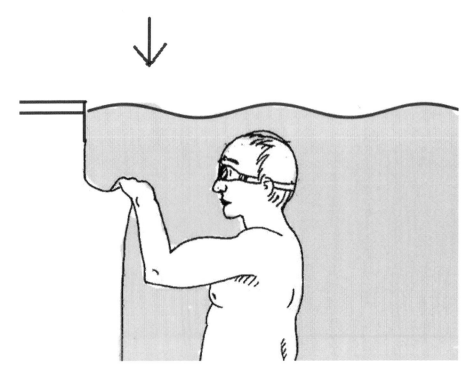

As always, practice a lot – in this case until you are able to submerge your whole head confidently and consistently. However, this stage should be much faster as you are building on your last skill, not starting a completely new one.

You should be feeling much more comfortable in the water now but remember to keep revisiting those previous skills like splashing water on yourself, sitting or lying on the steps or shallow ledge if you can and walking around in the shallow end. Do it with a smile and a sense of fun, you want your brain to register the water as something enjoyable, not an activity done with white knuckles.

Once you can confidently submerge your whole head for at least five seconds you are ready to move onto the next step.

CHAPTER CHECKLIST

★ Choose a pool that has an appropriate space for you to practice submersion – if not a pool, choose another vessel appropriate to practice

★ Find a time when the space is not crowded and generally not busy

★ Work your way up from mouth, mouth/nose, face and then whole head under the water

★ Use a nose clip or block your nose if you need to

★ Keep your mouth closed at this stage

★ Revisit previous skills

BUBBLING UP

I think I can, I think I can!

THE LITTLE RED ENGINE

BEAUTIFUL BUBBLES

Now that you can confidently put your head under the water you are ready to move onto bubbles. Many people have the idea that bubbles are just a fun component of swimming that we teach kids, but they are actually one of the cornerstones of a becoming a proficient swimmer. If you learn how to do bubbles now, they will become a natural part of your swimming and will help you enormously and save you time when you move onto formal swimming strokes. Learning how to blow bubbles in the water will also keep your heart rate down, keeping you more relaxed.

Do not skip this step! Work on it until it is comfortable and you can do it confidently and consistently. You know it, this may take some time, but the more time you put into it the faster you will improve. If you get into the habit of blowing bubbles now, it will soon become second nature and you won't have to consciously think about it.

Learning bubbles can be done in the same place as the previous step. So either head to the pool, fill your water vessel, jump into the bath or into the wading pool and get started.

Why do we need to blow bubbles? Because it is how we exhale in the water. Theoretically you don't <u>have</u> to blow bubbles – you can just hold your breath when you are under the water. However, if you do that, when you come to the surface to breathe you will need to first exhale and then inhale – which will require a longer interval with your head out of the water. Besides that, breath holding can get quite exhausting after a while. Try it while you walk, instead of exhaling, hold your breath until you run out of air. Now quickly exhale, then inhale and hold your breath again. I can guarantee you won't make it too far without getting out of breath. The same applies when you're in the water, when you're submerged you want to exhale your air by blowing bubbles. When you're above the water you want to inhale enough to keep you submerged for a reasonable time.

Try your first bubbles with just your mouth in the water (in a sitting/standing position if in the pool). Blow a gentle stream, (like you are blowing out a candle) then stop and take a rest. Concentrate on exhaling only and keep your bubbles small in a gentle stream. You want your bubbles to be relaxed, like you are exhaling while going for a stroll. You don't want to blow a torrent of big bubbles like a volcano as this will expel all your oxygen too fast.

Remember, you will only ingest water if you inhale while submerged. If you are scared of swallowing water, first and foremost remind yourself if won't hurt you. Obviously I don't recommend drinking vast quantities of non-potable water, but a couple of gulps will not harm you. With that in mind, progress as slowly as you need to. Start out at two seconds and progress up to at least five or seven seconds. If you do end up swallowing some water, just sit back, take a few deep breaths, compose yourself and try again. If you really concentrate on exhale only, it will be difficult to ingest any water.

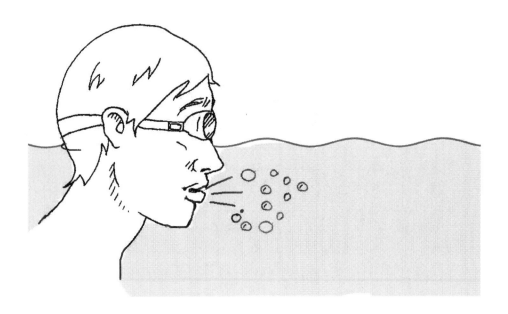

When you are <u>completely comfortable</u> with blowing bubbles with just your mouth under, move onto facial submersion with bubbles. Do just as you did with facial submersion before, but this time add in bubbles. Start at two seconds and move up to at least five. Remember exhale only! When you have conquered that move up to whole head submersion with bubbles and repeat the process.

Yes, once again, you need to practice this relentlessly. Just keep doing it over and over again until you are confident. It may take you two sessions, or it might be ten. Don't put yourself under any time pressure, just keep chipping away. There is no other way to become proficient. Sometimes adult students will say to me that kids pick up things much quicker. While it is true that physically children have advantages over adults when learning to swim, the other major advantage they have is that they are prepared to repeat a skill until they can do it and they don't give up when they have a setback (like swallowing water). They just dust themselves off and try again. Try and adopt that attitude and your progress will be much faster.

For those of you still holding your nose or using a nose clip, I recommend that you leave blocking your nose behind at this stage. If you can confidently blow bubbles with your head under the water, you don't need to worry about getting water up your nose. It is very difficult to exhale out of your mouth and inhale through your nose at the same time! The secret is not to inhale, so if you start exhaling as soon as you go under, you will not be able to inhale at the same time. Start slowly without your clip or holding your nose and move at your own pace. I bet you will do this much easier than you thought.

The only way to get water up your nose is to inhale or to have it splashed up there (which can happen occasionally if you around people who are splashing) or if you are upside down under the water (this can happen when you are doing a somersault) or if you jump in with a lot of force (for example a bomb dive). In that situation water is forced up your nose due to the laws of physics. At this stage the only scenario likely to happen is inhalation as you will probably not be around splashing, doing somersaults or bomb dives.

Remember, too, that even if you do get water up your nose, it's not the end of the world. I agree it is not a pleasant sensation, but it won't cause you any long-term damage. All you need to do is clear your nostrils by blowing out with your mouth closed (just like blowing your nose). Or another option is to go back under water and blow nasal bubbles, which I am just about to explain now.

Nasal bubbles are exactly what they sound like, it is the process of blowing bubbles out of your nose. They are simple to achieve, just submerge and exhale out of your nose, just like you are blowing it. At first, do not blow mouth bubbles at the same time so you are isolating the skill. Keep your mouth closed and exhale out of your nose. Then simply stop before lifting your head out of the water (making sure you don't inhale until your head is out of the water.).

Yep, you need to practice nasal bubbles until they are second nature. At this stage of your progression, it really shouldn't take you too long. Practice this skill the same way you did your mouth bubbles, by dipping your head under the water or submerging your whole head while holding onto the side or your support person. If you are still finding it tricky to get the hang of nasal bubbles, some people find that humming under the water can help as it keeps the mouth closed and exhalation from the nose happens without you having to focus too hard on it.

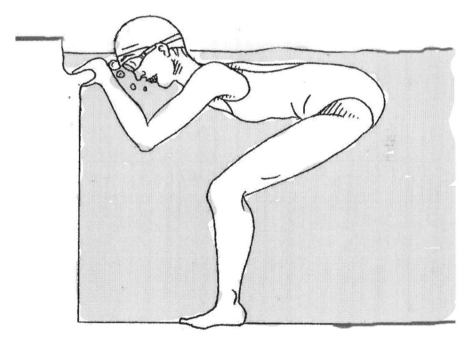

Note: *If you really cannot manage without your nose clip you can continue using it as you learn to swim. I honestly believe it is easier without it but don't let it be the reason that you don't progress in swimming. If you do keep using it, test yourself periodically and see if you can manage without it. You will probably surprise yourself. As I said before if you blow bubbles, it is very hard to inhale through your nose.*

Once you have the hang of nasal bubbles, you can use them in unison with mouth bubbles if you wish. Some people blow nasal bubbles only or others blow mouth bubbles only. Some people do both either in unison or mix it up a bit. It is a matter of personal preference and there is no right or wrong. As long as you are exhaling either through your mouth or your nose, or both, that is all that matters. If you are worried about getting water up your nose, blowing nasal bubbles is a great strategy as it eliminates that risk. Remember, as long as you are exhaling, no water can get in.

NEARLY THERE!

So, at this point you should be able to dip your whole head under the water and blow mouth and nasal bubbles for at least five seconds. (If you really want to speed ahead when you get to your formal class, keep practising until you can submerge for ten seconds or beyond. It's not as difficult as it sounds – you will be surprised just how quickly you progress as you gain confidence).

If you have been practising bubbles somewhere other than a pool, it is now time to head to a pool and give it a go. Use the earlier guidelines regarding shallowness in the pool and making sure you are stable before doing the same thing with your bubbles that you've been practising at home. It will take a little getting used to as chlorine can have a strong taste and smell (especially in an indoor pool). Make sure you have your support person with you as you adapt to being in the pool.

You can now combine your submersion/bubble blowing and moving around in the water. Walk around the pool (hang onto your support person if necessary) and practice bobbing up and down, blowing bubbles under the water, popping up for a breath and then submerging again. Although you may not yet be confident to walk around unaided, the submersion should be confident. You can also move into deeper water if you are confident enough – make sure you have your support person and can hang onto the wall firmly.

Note – I don't recommend going to another kind of waterway at this stage (eg a river/lake/ocean) mainly because there are elements there you can't control, such as current, hidden hazards like submerged objects, temperature and water clarity. When you are completely confident in the pool you can move onto other water sources.

When you can confidently submerge numerous times in a pool and blow both mouth and nasal bubbles you are ready to go onto the next stage. (By confidently I mean you are able to bob your head up and down without gasping or spluttering, feeling anxious or needing to stop and wipe your mouth/face or take a long break between submersions).

Congratulations – you have made a giant leap forward in your journey in learning to swim! You should find the next part a little easier as you are no longer scared of getting your face wet or accidentally going under the water.

CHAPTER CHECKLIST

★ Bubbles are vital when learning to swim

★ You will only ingest water if you inhale

★ Start bubbles with the mouth only, keeping nose blocked if required

★ Work your way up from immersing mouth, mouth/nose, face, and then whole head under while blowing bubbles with the mouth

★ Remove nose clip if you can

★ Repeat process with nasal bubbles, keep mouth closed to begin with to isolate skill

★ Revisit previous skills

OTHER BASIC SKILLS

It's not about perfect. It's about effort. And when you bring that effort every day, that's when transformation happens. That's when change occurs.

JILLIAN MICHAELS

You are really on your way now. Submersion is honestly the most difficult part of overcoming a water fear. As I mentioned earlier in the book it is, hands down, the element that holds most people back when they contemplate swimming lessons. So now you can confidently submerge, the other elements of swimming are more fun, and you can start seeing real progress as you link each new skill together.

As I mentioned on the very first page of this book, my intention is not to teach you how to swim strokes, but to help you overcome a fear of the water and get you confident enough to take part in swimming lessons. I am now going to run through some other basic skills that will also stand you in good stead before you embark on lessons.

EXPERIMENT ON A NOODLE

Pool noodles (sometimes called woggles) are long cylinders of foam that are designed to aid flotation for children and adults alike. They are light, flexible, and portable and will give you a feeling of confidence in the water while you are still learning. They are inexpensive to buy (especially at places like Big W or K Mart) but most pools have a good supply of them and will probably hire or lend them to you. Noodles can become waterlogged and lose some of their buoyancy over time, so make sure you have a fairly new one that still feels soft and light and floats on the surface of the water.

Enter the shallow end of the pool safely and stand with both feet firmly on the bottom. Now take the noodle, bend it slightly and place it firmly across your chest and under your arms (with the ends pointing behind you). Walk in the water until it is at least chest deep, then slowly lean forward and lift your feet off the bottom by bending your knees. Hang there for a moment in the water with your feet up. (Make sure you have your support person with you to guide you and support you). It can be scary doing this for the first time, but once you realise that the noodle will hold you up, you will quickly become more confident. Even if you lean too far forward and your face or head ends up in the water it doesn't matter

73

because you are now able to submerge without freaking out. Lift your feet off the bottom and put them back down several times. Get used to the motion of lifting the feet up and be comfortable with it. Try doing some basic kicking motions with your legs if you can. (Have your support person demonstrate). It does not have to be proper kicking at this point, just move your legs a little. Also practice setting your feet back on the bottom and finding that stability.

If you are feeling confident, go into deeper water. Just keep walking until your feet can no longer touch the bottom and let the noodle hold you up. (You can use two noodles for extra support if you need to). Keep your support person close by and again have them demonstrate how to do some basic kicking motions to propel yourself through the water.

Explore Deeper Water

If you are confident enough and your support person agrees you are ready, you can explore some deeper water. Move along the side of the pool, holding on firmly with both hands. This in itself is a good exercise in exploring your buoyancy, as you will notice how easy it is to stay afloat with just your hands holding you up. When the water is just over your head drop under the water (while holding onto the side) and see if you can touch the bottom with your feet. If you can, simply touch your feet on the pool bottom and then push back up. Remember to blow bubbles while you are submerged. You will notice how easily your body bobs back up to the surface. If you are comfortable at that depth, go a little further (of course still with your support person by your side). This time just leave your fingertips on the edge of the pool and drop yourself down until your feet touch the bottom and bob back up. Again, feel how easily your body floats back up.

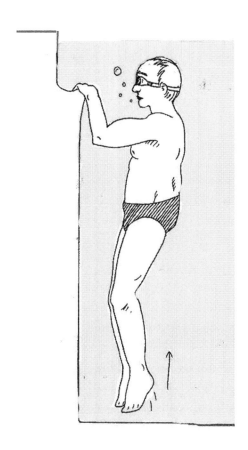

Here's a little secret about deep water, rather than wanting to drag you down, it wants to push you back up. The trick is being relaxed, and, as I previously mentioned, controlling your breathing is the easiest way to relax your body. Consciously take slow, even breaths until you feel calm. If you can get yourself in a relaxed enough state with the aid of your support person, exploring your buoyancy in deeper water can be a huge step forward in learning to swim. Practice this as often as you can, and you will be surprised how quickly you gain confidence.

OTHER FLOTATION DEVICES

I generally don't recommend the use of any other flotation devices – be it arm bands (Floaties), inflatable rings, buoyancy belts or life jackets when learning to swim. This goes for both children and adults. These devices will only teach you to rely on an object for buoyancy instead of using your own. Furthermore, they will make you develop an awkward and incorrect swimming style as different parts of your body will be artificially buoyant. The only exception to this would be if you have some kind of physical disability that prevents you from using your arms and legs fully in the water. The benefit of using foam noodles is that they give enough flotation to help you take that first step of finding your buoyancy but not enough to become overly dependent on them.

FLOATING

Floating is the cornerstone of all swimming strokes, both on your front and back. The good news is it is not too difficult for most people. You will need your support person to practice and two noodles (if possible).

I know for some adults the idea of lifting your feet off the pool bottom is just as challenging as submerging. It is a big leap in faith because you have to trust that the water will hold you up. If you have had previous experiences where you have sunk like a stone in the water, it is understandable that you will be sceptical about learning this skill.

It is true that some people float better than others. As I mentioned earlier heavier people tend to float very easily and women generally tend to be more buoyant than men. All in all, though, learning to float is about getting the correct body position and remaining calm and relaxed.

With floating your aim is to have a **horizontal** body position in the water. This means that your head needs to be flat with eyes looking down (the water should be lapping around your ears) and your legs and feet need to be as close to the surface as possible. Correct head position is the key here. As soon as you lift your head (even slightly) your hips (and legs) will drop and you will start to sink. Your hips will also have an impact on your float. If you allow your bottom to drop down (like a banana) you will force your head up and once again you will start to sink. If you feel your hips dropping, push them upwards. It may feel exaggerated when you are first learning, but you will soon learn the position that works best. Think about a float in simple physics terms. A boat cannot remain on the surface if one of the ends is higher than the other or if the hull starts to droop.

Your ability to float is substantially diminished when you tense your muscles to any degree. I tell kids when I'm teaching them that they need their body to feel like jelly – nice and loose. You have your support person next to you and they will not let you sink.

If you have access to a pool with a beach style entry or a shallow ledge, this is a perfect place to get a nice, gentle introduction to floating. First lie on your back in the shallowest area with your head on the bottom and the water up to your ears. Now lift your legs so they are floating on the surface (this will probably only be about ten centimetres). Just lie there for a while and get used to the sensation of your feet floating. Imagine that there are floats attached to your feet pulling them up to the surface. Once you can do the feet float confidently, move down a little bit deeper. Instead of lying with your head on the bottom lean back on your elbows and once again lift your feet off the bottom so they are floating on the surface of the water. Practice until you can do this confidently. This is something you can also practice in a wading pool or the bath (if it is big enough).

BACK FLOAT

A back float is easier to start with (as you don't have to put your face in the water). Stand in shallow water (around waist depth) and have your support person gently lower you onto your back. This is done by you crouching until neck deep and then slowly laying your head back while your support person supports your head and shoulders. As your head goes back, push your feet to the surface, making sure to push your hips up as well. Your eyes should be looking up. Extend your arms out wide. Once in position you can lie in the water with the aid of your support person.

If you have noodles, get your support person to position one under your neck and the other under your lower back. This will keep you afloat provided that you relax and just lie there. (As soon as you tense up or move too much your floating will be compromised). When using noodles, to begin with you can have your support person cradle your head with their hands, but as soon as you are comfortable allow them to gently remove their hands. Now just lie there for a minute or two and get used to sensation of floating. It really is very relaxing and peaceful.

As you get more confident doing this and feel your own buoyancy, you can gradually remove the noodle support. Take the back one away first and then the neck. When you are attempting your first float without noodles, have your support person support your shoulders and neck/head. Make sure your legs are on the surface of the water and push your belly button (hips) upwards. As long as you feel confident and if your support person believes you are ready, have them gradually reduce their shoulder support, then neck/head. Remember stay relaxed and you should maintain the float. Don't despair if you immediately sink – this is a skill that can take some time and patience. Go back a step and keep practising until it works.

Another way you can practice a back float is to hug a kickboard to your chest. Have your support person assist you into floating position and then place a kickboard on your chest. Encircle it with your arms (like a hug) and hold it there. Once you are comfortable your support person can let go. Concentrate on keeping your head flat in the water and your feet on the surface. If you are confident enough, you can try and get in position by yourself. Stand in waist to chest depth water holding the kickboard to your chest. Now, simply lean back slowly until you are lying back in the water.

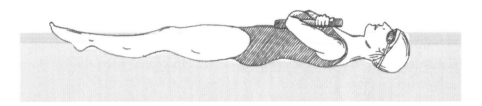

Once you have finished your back float, you need to get yourself back to an upright position. When you are first learning, this can feel scary and awkward as it is probably not something you have ever experienced before. The key to getting back upright is to bend your knees up towards your abdomen, which will then raise your head back up into an upright position and let you put your feet back down on the bottom. Doing this is moving your centre of gravity, so it does take some learning. Like I said, this can feel scary to begin with, so run through it slowly with your support person. Take your time, there is no rush. You will get better at it as you practice. Don't worry if you mess it up a few times, just keep thinking, bend the knees and head goes up. If you are using a kickboard, this can be done still holding onto the kickboard.

FRONT FLOAT

A front float is only more difficult because it involves having to lift your head and breathe, the physics is the same. You want your body to be horizontal in the water and your eyes looking to the bottom of the pool. This is very important. Having your eyes look down will keep your head (and the rest of your body) in the correct position. As soon as you look forward instead of down your hips will start to drop. If you get into the habit of putting your eyes to the bottom now you will save yourself a huge amount of time and effort as you progress through swimming. Having a correct body position is truly the cornerstone of swimming efficiently and having your head in the right place is the foundation for this.

Like the back float, there is a gentle way to start out. If you have access to a beach style pool or a pool with wide, flat steps or a shallow ledge, you can start your float there. Simply rest on your elbows or hands with your head out of the water. Allow your feet to rise to the surface and let them float there. Get your support person to help you if you need it and then try again by yourself.

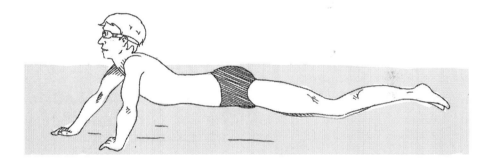

To start your float in the main pool, use the side of the pool to help you. Standing in the shallow end, extend your arms out straight and grasp the edge (or rail) firmly with both hands. Then take a breath and lower your face into the water with eyes looking to the bottom and blowing bubbles. Next get your support person to help you push your legs up to the surface and hold them there as long as you can. Providing your eyes look to the bottom and you keep your arms straight, your feet should stay on the surface. Once in the float, you can lift your head to take a breath and put it back in the water. To drop your feet back down again, bend your knees first up towards your abdomen and then push them back down to the bottom of the pool.

After a few assisted practices, try to push your legs up by yourself. Don't despair if you can't do it first try, be patient and persistent. Keep trying until you can do it, no matter how many attempts it takes. Remember, holding onto the wall will anchor you and keep you stable.

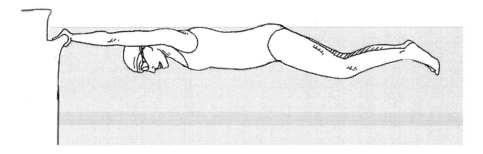

Once you have mastered the float holding onto the side, practice one with your support person. Grasp them firmly by the wrists, then place your head into the water and make sure your eyes look to the bottom. Blow bubbles as soon as your face goes into the water. Now, keeping your arms straight, push your legs up to the surface like you just practiced. Keep your face in as long as you can. When you've run out of air, simply lift your head up to take a breath and continue the float. Like holding onto the side, to return to the upright position, bend your knees towards your abdomen and lower your feet to the bottom

If you feel confident enough, you can let go of your support person while in the front float position. Just gradually let go of their wrists once you are in position the front floating position. Keep your arms straight out or move them out to right angles with your body. Keep blowing bubbles and stay relaxed and loose. You may surprise yourself how easily you can do an unassisted float. If you don't quite manage it on the first time, you know what you have to do – keep trying. Another way to transition is to hold a noodle out in front of you while you float. This will give you less stability than someone holding your wrists but will still provide some extra buoyancy. It will also allow you to practice putting your feet back on the bottom.

KICKING

Kicking is another core skill in swimming. If you take the time and effort to get it the basics right at this stage, you will surge ahead as you move through your swimming lessons. Kicking can prove challenging for adults, and you will probably never get as good as kicking as a child or adolescent would, but like any other physical skill, if you break it down it is achievable. The main thing about kicking is that it requires an awareness of what your legs are doing. If you understand what you need to do before you start learning you have a far greater chance of success than just having a go by yourself.

Kicking does not have to be hard and fast! Especially when you are first learning. Many adults do what is called a two-beat kick, which is a slower, less regular kick. This two-beat kick is enough to keep them moving in the water. Many distance swimmers use this kick as it is a good way to conserve energy when you have to swim a long way. You can think about the kick in freestyle like the back wheels of the car – they are necessary, but they don't do most of the work. It is your stroke that will move you through the water more than your kick.

The kick I am describing here is what is called a flutter kick. It is what is used when swimming freestyle or backstroke and is basically your legs moving up and down. When kicking either on the back or the front you need to kick from the hip down (not the knees). Your legs should be as straight as possible but not rigid. There should be some flexibility in your knees. A correct kick flows on from the horizontal body position. Once again you will need to have your head flat in the water (for both front and back kicking). This will keep your hips and legs on the surface of the water.

To start with, sit on the edge of the pool with your legs in the water. Then simply move your legs up and down in a kicking motion. Keep them fairly straight and kick from the hip. Point your toes like a ballerina. Practice this motion several times before moving onto the next stage. You can also sit in very shallow water, lean back on your hands and kick your legs up and down. Focus on a fairly straight, whole leg kick with pointed toes.

BACK KICK

Starting on your back is easier as you don't have to worry about breathing. Lying on your back in the water with your head flat and eyes up, grasp a kickboard onto your chest by wrapping your arms around it in a hugging fashion. Point your toes like a ballerina and work on a slow, whole-leg kick, making sure your feet are creating a small splash on the surface of the water. If you cannot feel the splash, your feet are not high enough. Ask your support person if you are doing the kick correctly. Go as slowly as you need to. Keeping your legs as straight as possible is key. If you are bending your knees, go back to sitting on the side and practising until you really get the hang of a whole leg kick from the hip down.

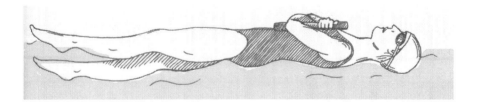

FRONT KICK

Start by holding onto the side firmly with both hands. Your arms should be straight and fully extended. Take a breath, lower your face in and make sure your eyes look to the bottom. Start blowing bubbles as soon as your face goes in. Then push your legs to the surface and start kicking. Take it slowly and concentrate on kicking from the hip down with your legs as straight as possible. Have your support person analyse your kick and tell you if you are bending your knees. If you are, go back to sitting on the side and focusing on a long, straight leg with pointed toes. After practising more, try again.

Once you can kick confidently while holding onto the side, you can try kicking on a kickboard. A kickboard is a rectangular piece of foam with a rounded top. Hold onto the square end with your fingers on the top and thumbs underneath. Lean forward in the water and put your face under the water, making sure you look to the bottom. Start blowing bubbles as soon as your face goes under. Then push off from the bottom and start kicking, remembering once again that you need to kick from the hip down and keep your legs as straight as possible. Push your bottom to the surface and adopt a slightly pigeon-toed foot position for the best result. You should feel your feet splashing on the surface of the water. Your support person can help you with this by holding onto the kickboard and keeping it stable until you get the feel of it. You can also do this with a noodle instead of a kickboard.

Kicking on a kickboard is actually quite challenging, especially if you have never done it before. Just practice it over a shorter distance and get the action right, rather than trying to go a long way.

One final skill you can work on before starting lessons is called the streamline. It is the position you begin all strokes in (although with backstroke it is on your back). Have you ever watched a swimming race on TV? When the swimmers dive in they are in the streamline position because it is the best possible way to gain forward momentum in the water.

The streamline position is not overly difficult to achieve, but like all the skills you have learned so far it will need some practice to get used to it. You will need to be comfortable with submersion and be able to kick to perform the streamline. You can actually practice the streamline on dry land before you try it in the pool. In fact, this is a good idea if your shoulders are not very flexible. Although the first few attempts may feel quite challenging, the more you repeat it, the more your shoulders should start to loosen up a bit. When children are learning this skill, I will make them stand in the streamline position on dry land and do it perfectly before they get into the pool. It is a great way to really drill it into muscle memory.

The streamline in the water involves having your arms extended straight in front of you, with your arms pressing against your ears and your head tucked down with your chin towards your chest. Your hands should be flat with one pressed on top of the other. Your legs should be long and straight. And it goes without saying that your eyes should be looking to the bottom.

To begin, stand with your back against the wall in the shallow end. Lift one foot and place it flat against the pool wall. As you lean down into the water, get your arms in position and then, once you are submerged, use the foot on the wall to push yourself forward and glide as far as you can holding the streamline position. Make sure you are blowing your bubbles as you glide. You will probably be surprised how far you will go. You will need to get back to the wall to go again, as you need that push to help you glide. Practice this until you are confident with it and then you can introduce kicking. Start the same way with one foot against the wall, but this time, start kicking as soon as you push off the wall. Go as far as you can while kicking, making sure your eyes are looking to the bottom and you are blowing bubbles. Your support person can direct you and point out any errors. Practice over a short distance. You will soon start to get the hang of it and when you are ready to move onto formal strokes, it will help you no end.

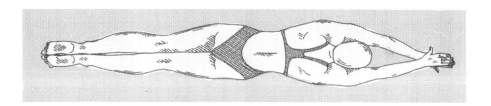

Aerial view of the streamline position.

CHAPTER CHECKLIST

★   Use a noodle to explore deeper water

★   Floating is the foundation of all swimming strokes

★   To float on the front or back maintain a horizontal body position and keep the eyes looking up (on your back) and to the bottom of the pool (front)

★   A flutter kick starts at the hip and uses the whole leg in a mainly straight position

★   Practice kicking on the front and back

★   The streamline position is the first building block for learning formal swimming strokes and is not difficult to do

★   Revisit previous skills

ENROLLING FOR LESSONS

Inaction breeds doubt and fear. Action breeds confidence and courage. If you want to conquer fear do not sit at home and think about it. Go out and get busy.

DALE CARNEGIE

Even though you may now be confident to submerge, float, kick and have a basic feel for the water, enrolling in lessons can still be a daunting prospect. I understand why you may feel that way but would like to assure you it doesn't need to be. Swimming teachers are trained to help you reach your goal and believe me; we love seeing people go from fear to love of the water. We do not laugh or make fun of anybody of any age who is brave enough to want to learn to swim (if you did come across such a teacher then you should report them to pool management).

Before committing to any kind of lessons I really urge you to do some research. Check out the pools in your area. Obviously it is more convenient to enrol in a pool that is very close by, but if you find a program that suits your needs a little better a bit further afield you should really consider enrolling there. You want to do everything you can to succeed, so don't let a bit of a drive put you off (if it comes down to that). Or you may find a mobile teacher willing to come to a private pool and conduct lessons there. This can be a great option if you or somebody you know has a pool that they are willing to let you use.

You can start by ringing swim schools and asking them about the lessons they offer. Talk to the swimming lesson co-ordinator rather than just a general pool employee if possible. Or perhaps you could email a list of questions to make sure you cover all the things you'd like to know. Also look at the pool website (almost all will have one) and see what information you can find there.

Next you should visit the pool(s) you are considering. Go at a time when there are lessons in progress and watch. You should be able to get a feel for the learning environment (as well as the actual pool itself). If you believe it will be a good fit for you ask about a trial lesson. Some pools don't charge for this, some do. But you should definitely be able to undertake a lesson without committing to a long-term program. If you are considering more than one swim school have trail lessons at all of them – there is nothing to say you can't do this.

Once you've had your lesson do some analysis about how it went. First of all, did you like the instructor? Did you think they were supportive and encouraging? Did you get along well with them? If you did and would like to continue your lessons, then go for it and enrol! Remember this has been a goal for a long time and you have now reached it. Well done! Enjoy the lessons and remember to keep practising regularly out of lesson time as well (it's simple maths, the more you practice the faster you will progress).

If the lesson didn't go as well as you hoped, please don't give up yet! Ask yourself what the problem(s) were. Was it an environmental factor? Was the centre too noisy or crowded? If so, schedule a lesson at a different time. Maybe you could consider an early morning or late afternoon/early evening lesson time. If the pool itself wasn't to your liking, you could give yourself a time frame – say five or ten lessons. If you still aren't comfortable there, then perhaps another centre might suit your needs better.

Was the problem with the instructor? Don't be afraid to admit if it was. I totally understand that some people 'click' better with one teacher than another. Perhaps you felt they were a little 'gung-ho' for your liking and you would like somebody quieter. Or perhaps it was the opposite – you would like somebody a bit more gregarious to push you harder. Maybe it's just a simple personality clash. Talk to the swimming lesson co-ordinator and explain your thoughts. They should be able to match you with somebody who will suit your needs better. Don't worry about offending anybody – the important thing is your progress and you need to do whatever you can to make your lessons work for you.

HOW OFTEN?

Once you have found yourself the right instructor in the right swim school, you will need to consider how often to have a lesson. As you have no doubt guessed, I am very much a believer in lots of practice as often as possible. This doesn't have to equal a lot of lessons (but it will require you to practice yourself outside lesson time).

The very least you should aim for is one lesson per week – any less than that and your skills may start to regress in the 'off' period between lessons. Two lessons per week is great and you will notice how quickly you start to improve. Three lessons (if you can manage it) is fabulous and will have you on the journey to swimming independently at a much faster rate. I know this can add up in terms of cost, but many swim schools offer a discount for multi-weekly lessons. The other thing to remember is that you can have more lessons in the early stages and less as you progress.

As mentioned above though, extra practice between lessons will help speed things up. Work on the skills you are learning and aim to get them down pat as fast as you can. If you can practice at least twice a week outside lesson time you will really notice a much faster rate of progression through lessons. In saying that though any practice is good, be it daily, weekly or monthly.

You Did It!

Congratulations, you've done it! You've gone from being a non-swimmer with a fear of the water to a student who is on the way to learning how to swim. You looked your fear in the face and pushed through. If you still feel like you haven't overcome your fear, keep trying. Continue to practice the early steps until submersion feels natural and then move onto floating and kicking. I have worked with swimmers who have taken a whole year to get comfortable but once they did, there was no stopping them.

If you stick with it and practice hard you <u>will</u> become a competent swimmer who can enjoy the water with their family and friends or use it as a way to exercise and relax.

Thank you for purchasing my book – I sincerely hope it has helped you overcome your fear and unlocked your swimming potential. I love feedback, so please feel free to drop me a line at katieswimguides@yahoo.com.au or leave a message on my Facebook page.

ABOUT THE AUTHOR

I am a lifelong lover of swimming! Right from my first introduction to the water I couldn't get enough of it. In saying that, though, I was very much a self-taught swimmer. Although my school did have a swimming program, it was much more basic than the ones offered today. There was only so much one teacher could do when faced with 30 kids of varying ability in one big group! Those were still the days of (some) parents and teachers believing that the best way for a child to learn to swim was to be thrown into deep water. While it may have worked for a select few, many children developed a fear of the water that they have carried on to adulthood.

Having seen my own mother miss out on a lot of family fun because she couldn't swim, I have long had a passion for encouraging non-swimmers to overcome their fear of the water and learn to swim.

Working in a stressful full-time job (in corporate finance), I often thought about using my passion for the water and swimming to become a swimming teacher. I knew it wasn't a full-time option, but when the opportunity came for me to reduce my work hours I did my teacher training and started teaching swimming part time. I love it and being a Learn To Swim teacher is the perfect anti-dote to the other stresses in my life. I am especially committed to helping adults achieve their swimming goals, not matter what stage of the learning journey they are at.

Happy Swimming!

Katie Smith

CONTACT INFORMATION

Website: www.theswimguide.weebly.com

Email: fitmates@yahoo.com.au

Facebook: www.facebook.com/TheSwimGuideAU

Other Publications

Adults Guide To Better Swimming

Helpful Ways To Improve Your Child's Swimming Skills

Printed in Great Britain
by Amazon

27191157R00056